WEALTH
&
PERCEPTION

The Intersection of Money and Mindset

Ujunwa Julieth Arua

ISBN: 9798393231484

DEDICATION

This book is dedicated to God Almighty for his inspiration and to my family for their support

CONTENTS

Introduction

1   Understanding Wealth

2   Perception of Wealth

3   Factors Influencing Perception

4   Wealth Illusion

5   Achieving Wealth and Perception Balance

6   Conclusion

Introduction

Wealth is a concept that has been the subject of countless discussions and debates for centuries. It is often perceived as a measure of financial abundance and material possessions. However, the true meaning of wealth goes far beyond this narrow definition. Wealth surrounds all facets of life, including health, relationships, security, personal fulfillment, and happiness.

Perception is one aspect that plays a key role in wealth. How we perceive wealth can shape our attitude toward money and our ability to accumulate it. Perception can either be a great tool for achieving financial success or a significant barrier to it.

This Book, titled "Wealth and Perception," aims to explore the relationship between wealth and perception. It delves into the idea that wealth is not just about money but also includes one's mindset, behavior, and overall outlook on life. The book lay more emphasis on the importance of understanding and managing one's perception of wealth to achieve long-term financial feat.

The purpose of this Book is to provide readers with a fresh perspective on wealth and encourage them to rethink their approach to money. It offers practical advice and strategies to help readers shift their perception toward wealth, leading to greater financial prosperity. Whether you are looking to build wealth or simply want to develop a healthier relationship with money, this book is for you.

Chapter 1

Understanding Wealth

Wealth is a multifaceted concept that is difficult to define concisely. People may understand wealth in diverse ways depending on their background, experience, and values. However, at its core, wealth refers to the abundance of resources that individuals, families, or societies possess. These resources can include financial assets, property, investments, and other material possessions. In this chapter, we will explore the various forms of wealth and examine how different perspectives on wealth shape our understanding of it. We will also delve into how society perceives wealth and how these perceptions influence our behaviors and decisions.

Defining Wealth and Its Various Forms

As mentioned, wealth can refer to the abundance of resources that individuals or groups possess. However, wealth can take on many forms beyond just financial assets. Some of the various forms of wealth include:

1. Financial Wealth: This type of wealth refers to money and other financial assets, such as stocks, bonds, and investments. It is often the most widely recognized and measured form of wealth. Financial

wealth provides individuals with the means to achieve their financial goals, such as buying a home, funding education, or saving for retirement.

2. Physical Wealth: Physical wealth includes tangible assets like real estate, cars, and other material possessions. Physical wealth provides individuals with a sense of security and comfort, as well as a means to showcase their achievements.

3. Social Wealth: Social wealth refers to social connections, networks, and relationships that individuals can leverage to access resources and opportunities. Social wealth provides individuals with access to job opportunities, mentorship, and other forms of social support.

4. Intellectual Wealth: Intellectual wealth encompasses knowledge, skills, education, and creativity that individuals can leverage to create value and generate income. Intellectual wealth provides individuals with the means to solve problems, innovate, and compete in the global marketplace.

5. Emotional Wealth: Emotional wealth refers to the ability to experience positive emotions like happiness, joy, and contentment, which are

essential for a fulfilling life. Emotional wealth provides individuals with a sense of inner peace and happiness, as well as the ability to cope with life's challenges.

6. Spiritual Wealth: This type of wealth refers to a sense of purpose, meaning, and connection to something greater than oneself. Spiritual wealth provides individuals with a sense of fulfilment and purpose, as well as the ability to navigate life's ups and downs with grace and resilience.

It's worth noting that these forms of wealth are not mutually exclusive. For example, social wealth can help individuals gain financial wealth, and intellectual wealth can help individuals acquire physical wealth.

Different Perspectives on Wealth

Wealth can be viewed from various perspectives, each with its own set of values and beliefs. Here are a few examples:

1. Economic Perspective: From an economic perspective, wealth is primarily defined by financial resources and their potential to generate income. In this view, wealth is seen as a measure of success and a way to achieve financial security and independence.
2. Social Perspective: From a social perspective, wealth is seen as a way of gaining access to

resources and opportunities, such as education, healthcare, and social connections. In this view, wealth is viewed as a means to improve one's social status and well-being.

3. Environmental Perspective: From an environmental perspective, wealth is seen as a way to preserve and sustain natural resources, such as clean air, water, and land. In this view, wealth is viewed as a means to promote environmental sustainability and protect the planet.

4. Personal Perspective: From a personal perspective, wealth is defined by one's values, beliefs, and priorities. For some, wealth may mean having enough money to support a family, while for others, it may mean having the freedom to pursue their passions and interests.

How Wealth is Perceived in the Society

The perception of wealth in the society can significantly impact our behaviours and decisions. Here are a few examples of how wealth is perceived in society:

- **Wealth as a Status Symbol**: In many societies, wealth is seen as a status symbol that signals success, power, and prestige. Individuals with high levels of wealth may be seen as more desirable or respected and may have access to exclusive social circles and events.
- **Wealth as a Measure of Success**: As mentioned earlier, wealth can be seen as a measure of success

and achievement. In some societies, individuals who have accumulated a significant amount of wealth may be viewed as more successful and accomplished than those who have not.

- **Wealth as a Source of Power**: Wealth can also be viewed as a source of

Chapter 2

Perception of Wealth

Perception is the way we regard, understand, interpret, and make sense of the world around us. It is a subjective experience that varies from person to person. When it comes to wealth, perception plays a significant role in how we view money, how we make financial decisions, and how we feel about our financial situation. In this chapter, we will explore the concept of perception as a subjective experience, cognitive biases, and their role in shaping perception, and how perception affects our relationship with wealth.

1. Perception as a Subjective Experience

Perception is a subjective experience because it is influenced by our thoughts, beliefs, and emotions. Our experiences and cultural backgrounds also shape the way we perceive things. For example, two people can look at the same painting and have different perceptions of it. One person may see the beauty in the colors and brushstrokes, while another person may see the chaos in the composition. Similarly, two people can have vastly different perceptions of wealth.

The perception of wealth is not solely based on how much money a person has. It is influenced by their beliefs, values, and experiences. Some people view wealth as a symbol of success and power, while others view it as a burden or a source of stress. Some people may feel that wealth brings happiness and fulfillment, while others believe that it can lead to corruption and greed. Perception of wealth is also influenced by cultural and societal norms. In some cultures, wealth is viewed as a measure of a person's worth, while in others, it is considered taboo to flaunt one's wealth.

Perception of wealth can also be influenced by media and advertising. Advertisements often create a perception of wealth that is unattainable for most people. They depict luxury lifestyles and products that are associated with wealth, creating a desire to attain that lifestyle. Social media can also create a perception of wealth through curated images of perfect lives and luxury experiences. These images can make people feel inadequate and create a desire to attain that level of wealth.

2. Cognitive Biases and Their Role in Shaping Perception

Cognitive biases are forms of thinking that can alter our perception of reality. They are subconscious and can affect our decision-making processes. Cognitive biases can be particularly influential in shaping our perception of wealth.

One cognitive bias that can affect our perception of wealth is the availability heuristic. This bias occurs when we base our perception of the likelihood of an event or the frequency of an occurrence on how easily it come to mind. For example, if we hear about a celebrity who has lost their wealth, we may perceive that wealthy people are more likely to lose their money, even though this is not necessarily true.

Another cognitive bias that can affect our perception of wealth is the confirmation bias. This bias occurs when we seek out information that confirms our pre-existing beliefs and ignore information that contradicts them. For example, if we believe that wealthy people are selfish and greedy, we may seek out stories that confirm this belief and ignore stories that portray wealthy people in a positive light.

The framing effect is another cognitive bias that can affect our perception of wealth. This bias occurs when we make decisions based on how information is presented to us. For example, if we are presented with a choice between two investment options, one framed as a potential gain and the other as a potential loss, we are more likely to choose the option framed as a gain, even if the potential loss option may be more financially beneficial.

3. How Perception Affects Our Relationship with Wealth

Perception can have a significant impact on our relationship with wealth. Our perception of wealth can influence our financial decisions, our emotions, and our overall well-being.

If we perceive wealth as a source of stress and anxiety, we may avoid taking risks and making financial decisions that could improve our financial success.

Chapter 3

Factors Influencing Perception

In the previous chapter, we explored how perception is a subjective experience and how cognitive biases can shape our perception of wealth. In this chapter, we will delve deeper into the factors that influence perception, particularly cultural and social factors. Perception is a complex and multifaceted phenomenon that is influenced by a variety of factors. Cultural and social factors are two of the most significant factors that can shape our perception of wealth. Our cultural background, social status, education, and social networks can influence how we view money, how we spend and save it, and how we make financial decisions. By understanding the factors that influence our perception of wealth, we can gain a better understanding of our financial behaviours and attitudes and make informed financial decisions that align with our values and goals.

Culture and Perception

Culture plays a significant role in shaping our perception of the world around us. It includes shared beliefs, values, customs, and practices that are passed down from generation to generation. Culture can influence the way we view wealth and money, and how we use them.

In some cultures, wealth is viewed as a measure of success and is associated with prestige, power, and respect. For example, in many Asian cultures, saving and investing money are seen as essential for financial stability and success. In contrast, in some African cultures, wealth is viewed as a way to help others and is shared with the community.

Cultural values can also influence how we view spending and saving money. For example, in Western cultures, spending money on experiences and material possessions is often seen as a way to increase personal happiness and well-being. In contrast, in some Asian cultures, saving money is valued more than spending it.

Social Factors and Perception

Social factors such as social class, education, and social networks can also influence our perception of wealth. Our social status can affect how we view wealth and money, as well as our spending habits and financial decisions.

Research has shown that individuals from higher social classes tend to view money and wealth as a source of security and status. They are more likely to invest in high-risk financial products and take financial risks. In contrast, individuals from lower social classes tend to view money as a means of survival and are more likely to focus on saving and spending money on necessities.

Education can also influence our perception of wealth. Studies have shown that individuals with higher levels of education tend to view wealth as a product of hard work and effort. They are more likely to engage in financial planning and investment activities.

Social networks, including family, friends, and colleagues, can also influence our perception of wealth. Research has shown that we are more likely to adopt the financial behaviours and attitudes of our social network. For example, if our friends and family members value saving and investing money, we are more likely to adopt these behaviours.

Individual Factors and Perception

Individual factors such as personality, subjective experiences, and beliefs can play a significant role in shaping our perception of wealth. Each person's unique set of experiences, values, and beliefs can influence their attitudes towards money and wealth.

Personality is one factor that can shape our perception of wealth. Research has shown that individuals who score high on traits such as conscientiousness and openness tend to view money as a means to achieve long-term goals, such as financial security and stability. In contrast, individuals who score high on traits such as impulsiveness and sensation-seeking tend to view money as a means to achieve immediate gratification and pleasure.

Personal experiences can also influence our perception of wealth. For example, individuals who have experienced financial hardship may view wealth as a source of security and stability. In contrast, individuals who grow up in affluent households may view wealth as a means of maintaining their social status and power.

Beliefs and values can also shape our perception of wealth. For example, some individuals may believe that wealth is a result of hard work and effort, while others may view wealth as a result of luck or privilege. These beliefs and values can influence our financial behaviours and decisions.

Personal Factors and Perception

Personal factors such as age, gender, and income can also influence our perception of wealth. These factors can influence our attitudes toward money, how we spend and save it, and our financial goals and priorities.

Age is one factor that can shape our perception of wealth. Research has shown that older adults tend to view wealth as a means to achieve financial security and stability, while younger adults may view wealth as a means to achieve social status and prestige.

Gender can also influence our perception of wealth. Studies have shown that men tend to be more risk-taking in their financial decisions and are more likely to engage in high-risk investments. In contrast, women tend to be more conservative in their financial decisions and are more likely to focus on saving and long-term financial planning.

Income is another factor that can shape our perception of wealth. Individuals with higher incomes tend to view wealth as a means to achieve financial security and status. In contrast, individuals with lower incomes may view wealth as a means to achieve basic needs and survival.

Media and Wealth

Media can shape our perception of wealth in several ways. One of the most significant ways media influences our perception of wealth is through the portrayal of wealthy individuals in TV shows, movies, and news coverage. Wealthy individuals are often depicted as powerful, influential, and successful. They are shown living in luxurious homes, driving expensive cars, and wearing designer clothes. These images can create a perception that wealth is the key to a luxurious and successful lifestyle.

Media can also influence our perception of wealth by framing wealth in certain ways. For example, news coverage of successful entrepreneurs and business leaders may create a perception that wealth is the result of hard work, determination, and innovation. In contrast, news coverage of wealthy individuals who inherit their wealth may create a perception that wealth is a result of privilege and luck.

Advertising and Wealth

Advertising is another significant factor that can shape our perception of wealth. Advertisements often use images of luxury and extravagance to sell products and services. For example, car commercials may show a wealthy individual driving a luxurious car through the city, creating a perception that owning the car will make the viewer feel powerful and successful.

Advertising can also influence our perception of wealth by framing products and services as symbols of success and status. Luxury brands often use images of wealthy individuals wearing their products to create a perception that owning the brand's products is a symbol of wealth and success.

The Role of social media

Social media is another powerful tool that can influence our perception of wealth. Social media platforms such as Instagram, TikTok, and Facebook are often used by individuals to display their wealth and success. Influencers and celebrities often post images and videos of themselves living a luxurious lifestyle, creating a perception that wealth is the key to happiness and success.

Social media can also create a perception of "keeping up with the Joneses." Users may compare their own lives to the lives of others they follow on social media, creating a perception that they need to attain a certain level of wealth to be successful or happy. Media and advertising play a significant role in shaping our perception of wealth. Through the portrayal of wealthy individuals in TV shows, movies, news coverage, advertising, and social media, we are constantly exposed to messages and images about what it means to be wealthy and successful. By understanding how media and advertising can influence our perception of wealth, we can be more mindful of the messages we are exposed to and make informed decisions about our financial behaviors and attitudes.

Chapter 4

Wealth Illusion

Wealth is a highly sought-after commodity in our society, where we prize it as the ultimate symbol of success and happiness. Many people spend their entire lives working towards achieving financial prosperity, believing that it will bring them everything they ever wanted. However, the reality is that wealth is often an illusion that can lead to dissatisfaction and false perceptions of happiness.

Wealth illusion is a term used to describe the false perception that money can solve all problems and bring lasting happiness. It is an illusion because wealth is just a means to an end, a tool that can be used to achieve certain goals but not guarantee happiness. The primary reason people fall for this illusion is that they associate wealth with security, comfort, and social status.

The media plays a significant role in promoting and perpetrating the wealth illusion by constantly portraying the lives of the rich and famous as something to aspire to. With celebrity magazines, reality TV shows, and social media platforms, we are bombarded with images of the lives of the super-rich, depicted as paradigms of success, happiness, and fulfillment. However, the reality of their lives is often far from glamorous, characterized by loneliness, isolation, and anxiety.

The Impact of Wealth Illusion on Society and Individuals

The wealth illusion has far-reaching effects on society, influencing our economic systems, social structures, and cultural values. In a capitalist society, the pursuit of wealth is the driving force behind economic growth, and the accumulation of capital is seen as a measure of success. However, this narrow focus on wealth and profit can lead to ethical issues, such as corruption, exploitation, and injustice.

Moreover, the pursuit of wealth can create a social divide, where only a select few can access the benefits of abundance, while the rest struggle to make ends meet. This can result in a class-based society, where the rich get richer, and the poor get poorer. Such a society can breed envy, resentment, and social unrest, as we have seen in many countries. The impact of the wealth illusion on individuals is equally significant, leading to a range of psychological issues, including stress, anxiety, depression, and addiction. People who are driven by the illusion of wealth are often unable to enjoy the present moment, constantly worrying about the future and chasing after material possessions. They are more likely to experience burnout, lose focus on their relationships, and find themselves increasingly isolated from others.

Overcoming the Wealth Illusion

To avoid the wealth illusion, it is important to focus on the non-monetary aspects of wealth. These include relationships, personal growth, and experiences. It is also important to maintain a healthy perspective on money and not allow it to become the sole focus of one's life. To overcome the wealth illusion, we must first acknowledge its existence and the harmful effects it can have on our lives. We must recognize that true happiness and fulfillment are not linked to material possessions or social status but rather to our sense of purpose, connection, and self-worth. We must learn to appreciate and enjoy the present moment, cultivate meaningful relationships, and find ways to give back to our communities.

We can also take practical steps to reduce the hold that money has over our lives. For example, we can adopt a more minimalist lifestyle, where we prioritize experiences and relationships over material possessions. We can save money and invest it in our education, personal growth, or social causes that we believe in.

We can also find ways to use our wealth wisely, instead of using it to fulfill our immediate desires. For example, we can donate to charity, support social causes, or invest in sustainable development projects. By doing so, we can transform our relationship with money from one of obsession to one of responsibility and care for others and the planet.

The illusion of wealth is a pervasive and harmful concept that has become central to our economic, social, and cultural systems. It is an illusion because it can lead to false perceptions of happiness, emotional emptiness, and ethical issues. To overcome this illusion, we must learn to appreciate the present moment, cultivate meaningful relationships, and use our wealth wisely, only then can we create a society that values human connections and personal growth over material possessions and social status. It is necessary to realize that wealth is just a means to an end and not the end itself.

Chapter 5

Achieving Wealth and Perception Balance

Wealth and perception are two important aspects of life that are often intertwined. Many people strive to accumulate wealth as a means of improving their perception of society. However, the pursuit of wealth can sometimes lead to a skewed perception of oneself and others. In this chapter, we will explore how to achieve a balance between wealth accumulation and perception.

1. The Perception Trap

The perception trap is a common phenomenon where people become obsessed with how they are perceived by others. This can lead to a focus on accumulating wealth as a means of improving their perception. However, this pursuit of wealth can lead to a skewed perception of oneself and others. It can also lead to a loss of focus on other important aspects of life, such as relationships and personal growth.

To avoid the perception trap, it is important to focus on the intrinsic value of wealth. Wealth should be seen as a means to an end, not an end in itself. It is important to remember that wealth alone does not guarantee happiness or fulfillment. Instead, wealth should be used to create opportunities and experiences that enhance one's life.

2. Balancing Wealth and Perception

Achieving a balance between wealth accumulation and perception requires a multi-faceted approach. This includes focusing on the intrinsic value of wealth, avoiding the perception trap, and maintaining a healthy perspective on money. It also involves developing a strong sense of self-worth that is not dependent on external validation.

One way to achieve this balance is by setting goals that align with one's values. This includes both financial and non-financial goals. For example, a person may set a financial goal of saving a certain amount of money each year while also setting non-financial goals such as spending more time with family and friends.

Another way to achieve balance is by practicing gratitude. This involves being thankful for what one has rather than focusing on what one lacks. By focusing on the positives in life, one can develop a healthier perspective on money and wealth.

3. The Role of Mindset

Mindset plays a crucial role in achieving a balance between wealth accumulation and perception. A growth mindset involves a focus on personal growth and development rather than external validation. This mindset allows one to see failures and setbacks as opportunities for learning and growth.

In contrast, a fixed mindset involves a focus on external validation and a fear of failure. This mindset can lead to a focus on accumulating wealth as a means of improving one's perception. However, it can also lead to a loss of focus on other important aspects of life.

To develop a growth mindset, it is important to focus on personal development and learning. This includes seeking out new experiences and challenges, setting goals, and reflecting on one's progress.

- **Practical tips for achieving a healthy perception of wealth.**

Achieving a healthy perception of wealth requires a balance between wealth accumulation and perception. In the previous chapter, we explored the various aspects that contribute to achieving this balance. In this chapter, we will discuss practical tips for achieving a healthy perception of wealth.

1. Define Your Values

One of the most important steps in achieving a healthy perception of wealth is defining your values. Your values are the principles and beliefs that guide your life. They influence your decision-making, behaviors, and relationships. Defining your values helps you understand what is important to you, and what you want to achieve in life.

When defining your values, it is important to consider your goals and aspirations. What do you want to achieve in life, and how does wealth fit into those aspirations? Are you focused solely on accumulating wealth, or are there other things that are equally important to you?

Once you have defined your values, you can use them as a guide in making financial decisions. This helps ensure that your wealth accumulation aligns with your overall goals and aspirations.

2. Create a Budget

Creating a budget is an essential step in achieving a healthy perception of wealth. A budget helps you manage your finances and ensures that you are living within your means. It also helps you prioritize your spending and saves money for the things that matter most.

When creating a budget, it is important to be realistic about your income and expenses. Identify your fixed expenses (such as rent, utilities, and debt payments) and your variable expenses (such as food, entertainment, and travel). Determine how much money you have available for each category and allocate your resources accordingly.

Creating a budget helps you avoid overspending and accumulating debt. It also helps you develop a healthy perspective on money and understand the true value of your wealth.

3. Prioritize Experiences Over Things

In our consumer-driven society, it is easy to fall into the trap of valuing things over experiences. However, experiences are what truly enrich our lives and create lasting memories. Prioritizing experiences over things can help you develop a healthy perception of wealth.

Instead of buying the latest gadgets or luxury items, focus on experiences that enrich your life. This could be travel, spending time with loved ones, or pursuing a hobby. By prioritizing experiences over things, you can develop a deeper appreciation for life and what truly matters.

4. Practice Gratitude

Gratitude is a powerful tool for developing a healthy perception of wealth. Practicing gratitude involves being thankful for what you have, rather than focusing on what you lack. It helps you develop a positive perspective on life and appreciate the true value of your wealth.

To practice gratitude, take time each day to reflect on what you are thankful for. This could be as simple as being grateful for good health or a supportive network of friends and family. By focusing on the positives in your life, you can develop a healthier perspective on wealth and understand the true value of your resources.

5. Give Back to Others

Giving back to others is an important step in achieving a healthy perception of wealth. It involves using your resources to help others and make a positive impact in the world. By giving back, you can develop a sense of purpose and fulfillment that is not dependent on external validation.

There are many ways to give back, including volunteering, donating to charity, and mentoring others. Find a cause that aligns with your values and interests and get involved. By giving back, you can develop a sense of empathy and understanding for others and develop a deeper appreciation for the true value of your wealth.

- **Real-life examples of individuals who have achieved wealth and perception balance.**

Wealth and perception are two important aspects of a person's life. Wealth is often associated with financial success, while perception is associated with how others perceive a person's success. Achieving wealth and perception balance is crucial for one's overall success in life. we will discuss some real-life examples of individuals who have achieved wealth and perception balance.

- **Warren Buffett** is a well-known name in the world of finance. He is one of the most successful investors in the world, with a net worth of over $100 billion. However, he is also known for his simple lifestyle and frugality. Despite his immense wealth, he still lives in the same house he bought in the 1950s and drives a modest car. His perception is that he is a down-to-earth and humble person, which has helped him maintain a positive public image.

- **Oprah Winfrey** is another example of a person who has achieved wealth and perception balance. She is a media mogul with a net worth of over $2.7 billion. However, she is also known for her philanthropy and for using her wealth to help others. She has donated millions of dollars to various charities and has used her platform to raise awareness about social issues. Her perception is that she is a compassionate and caring person, which has helped her maintain a positive public image.

- **Elon Musk** is a visionary entrepreneur and the founder of companies such as Tesla, SpaceX, and PayPal. He is known for his innovative ideas and his ability to turn them into successful businesses. He is also known for his unconventional approach to business, which often involves taking risks that others would not. His perception is that he is a risk-taker and a visionary, which has helped him maintain a positive public image despite some controversial decisions.

- **Bill Gates** is another example of a person who has achieved wealth and perception balance. He is a co-founder of Microsoft and one of the richest people in the world, with a net worth of over $100 billion. However, he is also known for his philanthropy and for using his wealth to help others. He and his wife have donated billions of dollars to various charities and have used their foundation to fight diseases such as malaria and polio. His perception is that he is a philanthropist and a humanitarian, which has helped him maintain a positive public image.

- **Mark Zuckerberg** is the co-founder and CEO of Facebook, one of the most popular social media platforms in the world. He is known for his innovative ideas and his ability to create a product that has changed the way people communicate. However, he has also faced criticism for Facebook's handling of user data and for its role in spreading misinformation. His perception is that he is a brilliant entrepreneur, but also someone who needs to take responsibility for the negative aspects of his creation.

- **J.K. Rowling** is the author of the Harry Potter series, which has sold over 500 million copies worldwide. She is known for her creativity and her ability to create a world that has captured the imaginations of millions of people. However, she has also faced criticism for her comments on social media and her views on transgender rights. Her perception is that she is a talented author, but also someone who needs to be mindful of the impact of her words on others.

4. **Richard Branson** is the founder of the Virgin Group, a conglomerate that includes companies such as Virgin Atlantic and Virgin Galactic. He is

known for his adventurous spirit and his willingness to take risks. He is also known for his philanthropy and for using his wealth to help people.

Chapter 6

Conclusion

"Wealth and Perception" is an insightful book that examines the relationship between wealth and perception. The author has delved deep into the subject, presenting a detailed analysis of the ways perception affects wealth and how wealth affects perception. The book has been a great resource for anyone looking to understand the dynamics of wealth and perception.

In this concluding chapter, we will recap the key points discussed in the Book and offer final thoughts on the importance of the perception of wealth.

Recap of Key Points

1. Perception shapes our reality.

Perception plays a crucial role in shaping our reality. Our perception of wealth determines how we view money and how we choose to spend it. Our perception also affects how we view success, status, and overall well-being. Therefore, it is essential to understand how perception works and how it affects our lives.

2. Perception affects our financial decisions.

Our perception of wealth and money influences our financial decisions. People who view money as a tool to achieve their goals tend to make better financial decisions than those who view money as a source of happiness. Our perception of wealth can also influence how we invest and manage our money, which can have a significant impact on our financial well-being.

3. Perception affects our relationship with money.

Our relationship with money is influenced by our perception of wealth. People who view money as a means to an end tend to have a healthier relationship with money than those who view it as an end in itself. Our perception of wealth can also affect our spending habits, which can impact our financial well-being.

4. Wealth can affect our perception.

Wealth can also affect our perception. Wealthy people tend to view the world differently than those who are not. Wealth can create a sense of entitlement, which can lead to a distorted view of reality. Wealth can also affect our relationships, as people may view us differently because of our wealth.

5. Perception is not fixed.

Our perception of wealth is not fixed. It can change over time based on our experiences and the information we receive. We can also choose to change our perception of wealth by changing our mindsets and beliefs. Therefore, it is important to be aware of our perception of wealth and how it may affect our lives.

Final Thoughts on the Importance of Perception of Wealth

Perception is a powerful tool that can impact our lives in many ways. In the context of wealth, perception can affect our financial decisions, our relationship with money, and our overall well-being. It is important to understand how perception works and how it affects us to make informed decisions about our finances.

One of the key takeaways from this book is that our perception of wealth is not fixed. We have the power to change our mindset and beliefs about wealth, which can have a significant impact on our financial well-being. By changing our perception of wealth, we can become more financially responsible, make better financial decisions, and ultimately achieve our financial goals.

Another important point to note is that wealth is not the only measure of success. Our perception of success should not be limited to our financial status but should encompass our overall well-being, including our health, relationships, security, and personal fulfillment.

In conclusion, "Wealth and Perception" has been an enlightening read that has shed light on the relationship between wealth and perception. By understanding how perception works and how it affects our lives, we can make informed decisions about our finances and ultimately achieve our financial goals.

www.ingramcontent.com/pod-product-compliance
Lightning Source LLC
Chambersburg PA
CBHW070905220526
45466CB00005B/2137